VISIONS

Student Handbook

THOMSON
™
HEINLE

Australia ◊ Canada ◊ Mexico ◊ Singapore ◊ United Kingdom ◊ United States

THOMSON
* TM

HEINLE

VISIONS STUDENT HANDBOOK

Publisher: *Phyllis Dobbins*
Director of Development: *Anita Raducanu*
Director, ELL Training and Development: *Evelyn Nelson*
Developmental Editor: *Tania Maundrell-Brown*
Associate Developmental Editor: *Yeny Kim*
Associate Developmental Editor: *Kasia Zagorski*
Editorial Assistant: *Audra Longert*
Production Supervisor: *Mike Burggren*
Marketing Manager: *Jim McDonough*
Manufacturing Manager: *Marcia Locke*
Photography Manager: *Sheri Blaney*
Production Editor: *Samantha Ross*
Development: *Quest Language Systems, LLC*
Design and Production: *Proof Positive/Farrowlyne Associates, Inc.*
Cover Designer: *Studio Montage*
Printer: *Thomson/West*

Printed in the United States of America.
10   08   07

For more information, contact Heinle, 25 Thomson Place, Boston, Massachusetts 02210 USA,
or you can visit our Internet site at http://www.heinle.com

ISBN-13: 978-0-8384-5840-2
ISBN-10: 08384-5840-8

TABLE OF CONTENTS

VISIONS Student Handbook • Copyright © Heinle

TABLE OF CONTENTS (CONT...)

VISIONS Student Handbook • Copyright © Heinle

Listening and Speaking
How to Give an Oral Presentation

An **oral presentation** is when you speak to a group of people to explain, describe, or persuade.

Step 1. Plan your presentation.
1. Brainstorm ideas about what you want to say.
2. Make a list of the best ideas.

Step 2. Organize your presentation.
Use an outline or a graphic organizer to organize your ideas and put them in order.

> *Outline of Presentation on "Sports for All"*
> I. What is "Sports for All"
>   A. A group of teenagers and adults
>   B. Want more sports facilities
> II. Importance of sports in our community
>   A. For fun
>   B. For health

Step 3. Prepare your oral presentation.
1. On note cards, write a few key words or phrases for each idea.
2. Think of an interesting opening, for example, a question or something funny or dramatic.

> *Sports*
> *Important in our community*
> *Most people like some kind of sport*

> *You won't believe who I saw yesterday!*

Step 4. Prepare a visual.
1. Decide what visual would help your audience understand your topic better.
2. Prepare your visual. Use poster board or presentation software. Make it big enough for the entire audience to see.

Step 5. Practice your presentation.
1. Decide how you will use language and your voice. Should your language be formal or informal? Should your tone of voice be light or serious?
2. Decide how you will use your body. Will you sit or stand? What gestures can help the audience understand your points? Look at your audience most of the time.
3. Practice your presentation in front of a mirror, and then with someone else.
4. Use the Speaking Checklist on page 2, and ask the person who heard you to give you feedback.

Step 6. Give your presentation to your audience.
1. Be sure that you have your note cards and your visual.
2. Go over your opening in your mind. Take a deep breath and stand or sit up straight.
3. After your presentation, ask the audience to complete the Active Listening Checklist on page 3.

Speaking Checklist

Use this checklist to evaluate your speaking.

1. Did I speak too slowly, too quickly, or just right? _____

2. Was the tone of my voice too high, too low, or just right? _____

3. Did I speak loudly enough for the audience to hear me?   ____ Yes ____ No

4. Did I produce the correct intonation patterns of sentences?   ____ Yes ____ No

5. Did I have a good opening?   ____ Yes ____ No

6. Did I look at my audience?   ____ Yes ____ No

7. Did I speak with feeling?   ____ Yes ____ No

8. Did I support my ideas with facts and examples?   ____ Yes ____ No

9. Did I tell the audience how I feel about the topic?   ____ Yes ____ No

10. Did I use interesting, specific words?   ____ Yes ____ No

11. Did I use visuals to make the speech interesting?   ____ Yes ____ No

My Own Criteria

12. _____   ____ Yes ____ No

13. _____   ____ Yes ____ No

14. _____   ____ Yes ____ No

VISIONS Student Handbook • Copyright © Heinle

Active Listening Checklist

Use this checklist to evaluate how well you listen and understand.

1. I liked _____ because _____

_____

2. I want to know more about _____

_____

3. I thought the opening was interesting. ___ Yes ___ No

4. The speaker stayed on the topic. ___ Yes ___ No

5. I did not understand _____

_____

6. I needed the speaker to repeat or clarify _____

_____

7. My own criteria: _____

_____

8. My own criteria: _____

_____

9. My own criteria: _____

_____

Viewing and Representing

Viewing Checklist

Visuals help you understand texts and presentations better. Analyzing visuals for their usefulness will help you to learn how to create good visuals. Think about these points as you view and create visuals.

1. Do I understand the purpose of this visual? _____ Yes _____ No

2. What is the purpose? _____
_____

3. Does this visual help me to understand better? _____ Yes _____ No

4. How does it help me understand? _____
_____

5. Is the visual labeled clearly? _____ Yes _____ No

6. Does the visual give me extra information? _____ Yes _____ No

7. What did I learn from the visual? _____
_____

8. Would I create the same visual for this text/presentation? _____ Yes _____ No

9. What would I do differently? _____
_____

10. My own viewing criteria: _____
_____

11. My own viewing criteria: _____
_____

Reading

Reading Strategies

Reading strategies can help you understand, remember, and enjoy what you read.

Use the text structure or elements of literature as you read.	
Connect main ideas.	Understand dialogue to understand characters.
Connect themes.	Understand genre features.
Find supporting arguments.	Understand setting.
Identify cause and effect.	Understand tone.
Identify images.	Use chronology to locate and recall information.
Identify main ideas and supporting details.	Use graphic sources of information.

Use your own experiences and thoughts as you read.	
Analyze characters.	Draw conclusions with text evidence.
Analyze plot.	Make predictions.
Compare and contrast.	Make inferences with text evidence.
Distinguish facts from opinions.	

Organize and remember information as you read.	
Classify information.	Recall facts and details.
Describe features.	Represent text information in an outline.
Explain elements.	Summarize to recall ideas.
List steps in a process.	Visualize elements.
Paraphrase to recall ideas.	Scan for key information.
Read aloud to show understanding.	

The Writing Process

Steps in the Writing Process

The **steps in the writing process** will help you achieve your goals as a writer.

Step 1. Gather information and do research.
1. Write the general topic on a piece of paper. Brainstorm ideas for specific topics.
2. Choose one of the specific topics to write about.

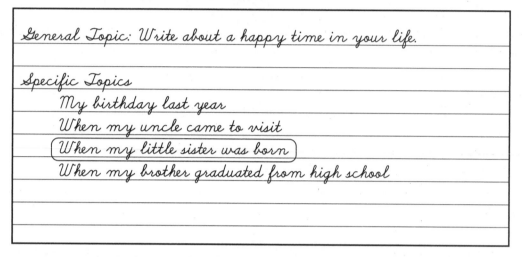

3. Brainstorm ideas about your topic. Use a web. See page 8. Write down your ideas. Choose the ideas that you think are the most important or interesting.
4. Sometimes you need to learn more about the topic by doing research. See pages 20 and 21 for more information on the research process.

Step 2. Organize your writing.
1. Use an outline or a graphic organizer such as a Venn Diagram, a Sunshine Organizer, or a timeline to organize your ideas from Step 1. See pages 8 and 9.
2. Decide what information you will include in each paragraph. The first paragraph should be an introduction. The final paragraph should be a conclusion. Organize your body paragraphs in a logical progression. You may want to use chronological (time) order or put the most important ideas first.

Step 3. Plan your writing.
1. Think about the purpose of your writing. Do you want to explain, persuade, or entertain?
2. Decide who your audience is. It could be your teacher, your classmates, or a larger group, such as everyone in your school.
3. Think about the text structure of your writing, for example, narrative, informational text, or biography. The text structure can help you decide what kind of information to include and how to organize it.

VISIONS Student Handbook • Copyright © Heinle

Step 4. Write a draft.

1. Use your ideas from Step 2 to write a draft. Think about the decisions you made about purpose, audience, and text structure in Step 3.
2. Do not worry about making errors at this point. Just work on expressing your ideas clearly.

Step 5. Edit your writing.

1. Edit your own work. Use the Editor's Checklist on pages 10 and 11. If you are writing on a computer, use the spelling and grammar checks. Make the changes in your draft. Blend and reorganize sentences and paragraphs.
2. Give your edited draft to a partner. Ask him or her to use the Peer Editing Checklist on page 12 to give you feedback.

Step 6. Revise your draft.

1. Look at the feedback from the Peer Editing Checklist. Make the changes that you agree with.
2. Make any other changes that are necessary.
3. Write a final copy in your best handwriting or on the computer.

Step 7. Proofread.

1. Read carefully to look for errors.
2. If you are using a computer, use the spell check, grammar check, or other software to check for errors. Print out a clean copy with correct paragraph indents and margins.
3. If you are writing by hand, you can correct a few small errors on the page. If you find a lot of errors, or if there is a major mistake, write out another copy.

Step 8. Publish.

1. Share your writing with other people. You can post it on a bulletin board. You can take it home for your family, or you can send it to your school newspaper. You can create a collection of student writing to share with another class.
2. Ask people for feedback on your writing. Find out what they liked. Find out how you can improve your writing.

Venn Diagram

Compare and Contrast

➤ Use a Venn Diagram for listening and speaking, writing, and viewing activities.

1. Write the two things you are comparing on the lines in the two circles.
2. List ways the two things are different under the lines.
3. List ways the two things are alike in the space where the circles overlap.

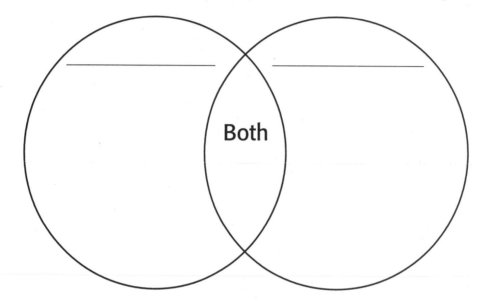

Web

➤ A Web is useful for building vocabulary or for a main idea and details.

1. Write the main vocabulary word or main idea in the large oval in the middle.
2. Write related vocabulary words or details in the smaller ovals.
3. Add or delete ovals as needed.

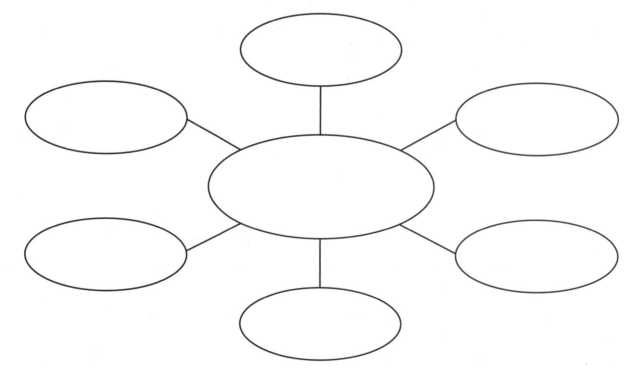

Sunshine Organizer

Reporting

➤ Use a Sunshine Organizer to help you answer questions about a story or to write a report.

1. Write the topic in the circle in the middle.
2. Write answers to the *wh-* questions next to the triangles.

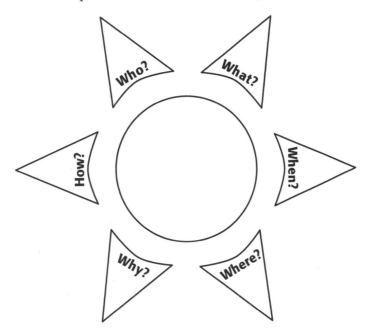

Timelines

➤ Select one of the timelines to show order of events.

1. Write the events in the order they took place.
2. On the left, write the first event and the date.
3. On the right, put the latest event and the date.

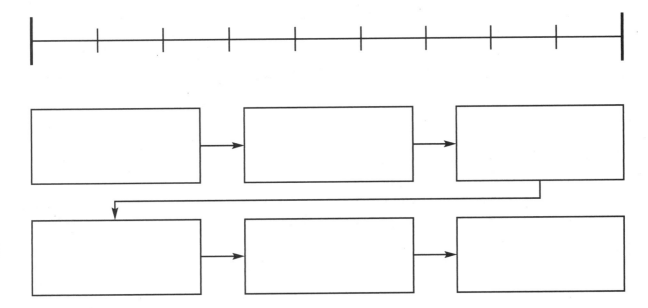

Editor's Checklist

Use this checklist to proofread and revise your writing. Make a check in the box when you have edited your writing for each item. Give this checklist to your teacher with your writing assignment.

Edit for:	Student Check ✔	Teacher Comments	Score
I. Development of Ideas/Content			
A. Is the purpose of my writing clear?	☐		
B. Is my writing focused on the topic I'm writing about?	☐		
C. Did I support my ideas with details, facts, and examples?	☐		
D. Did I write appropriately for my audience?	☐		
II. Organization			
A. Is my writing clear and logical?	☐		
B. Do I have a strong, interesting beginning that gets the reader's attention?	☐		
C. Are my ideas tied together? Do I use transitions?	☐		
D. Do I have a strong ending that ties things together?	☐		
III. Sentence Structure			
A. Are my sentences complete? Do they have a subject and a verb?	☐		
B. Did I make sure I don't have any run-on sentences or fragments?	☐		
C. Did I use different types of sentences — compound and complex?	☐		
IV. Grammar and Usage			
A. Is my writing in the right tense (for example, present or past)?	☐		
B. Did I use subject pronouns and object pronouns correctly — *I/me, he/him, she/her, we/us, they/them*?	☐		
C. Did I use the pronouns *she, her,* or *hers* for women and girls and *he, him,* or *his* for men and boys?	☐		
D. Do my verbs agree with their subjects? Did I use singular verbs with singular subjects and plural verbs with plural subjects?	☐		

➪

VISIONS THE WRITING PROCESS

VISIONS Student Handbook • Copyright © Heinle

10 VISIONS STUDENT HANDBOOK

Editor's Checklist (cont . . .)

Edit for:	Student Check ☑	Teacher Comments	Score

V. Word Choice
  A. Did I choose vivid and exact words? Did I use a thesaurus, glossary, or dictionary to help me choose better words?
  B. Did I eliminate extra words so that my writing is not wordy?
	☐
	
	☐		

VI. Writing Conventions
Form
  A. Did I write my name, the date, and a title on the page?
  B. Did I indent the first line of each paragraph?
  C. Did I include a bibliography and correctly cite any references that I used?
  D. Did I create an attractive computer presentation, or did I use my best handwriting?
Spelling
  E. Did I check the spelling of all words I'm not sure about?
  F. If I wrote my paper on a computer, did I use spell check?
Capitalization
  G. Did I capitalize the names of proper nouns, such as people's names and the names of cities and countries?
  H. Did I start each sentence with a capital letter?
Punctuation
  I. Did I punctuate each sentence with the right mark (., ?, or !)?
  J. Did I put quotation marks around any direct speech?
  K. Did I use apostrophes correctly in contractions and possessives?
	☐
	☐
	☐
	☐
	
	☐
	☐
	
	☐
	☐
	
	☐
	☐
	☐		

VII. My Own Criteria
  A.
  B.
  C.
	☐
	☐
	☐		

Peer Editing Checklist

Use this checklist to edit your peer's writing.
You may also use it to check your own writing.

Writer's Name _____

Editor's Name _____

1. Is there a title? _____ Yes _____ No

2. Is the first sentence of each paragraph indented? _____ Yes _____ No

3. Does each sentence start with a capital letter? _____ Yes _____ No

4. Does each sentence end with a punctuation mark? _____ Yes _____ No

5. Does each name start with a capital letter? _____ Yes _____ No

6. Write one correct sentence from the paper.

   _____

7. Write one sentence that has a mistake.

   _____

8. Rewrite the sentence correctly.

   _____

Use these editing symbols:

¶	Start a new paragraph.
∧	Insert a word or words.
Sp	Correct a spelling error.
CAP	Use a capital letter.
lc	Use a lowercase letter.
p	Correct a punctuation error.
exact	Use a more exact word.
?	What does this mean?
∽	Transpose these letters.

Responding to Peers' Writing: *EQS*

E: Encourage	*Q*: Question	*S*: Suggestions
• Help your partner recognize what he or she is doing right. • Be specific. Say things like: "I liked the surprise at the end the best." "You used some very interesting words in this sentence." "This poem made me think of my home."	• Ask questions when you would like more information. • Ask questions when something isn't clear. For example: "Why did your grandmother give you that picture?" "What do you mean, 'He went back'? Where did he go?"	• Ask your partner if he or she would like some suggestions. If your partner says "yes," offer suggestions to make the writing better. • Always let your partner choose whether or not to use your ideas. • Don't tell your partner what to do. Instead, make suggestions like: "You might try saying, 'My dog is fat' another way. How about 'my dog looks like a sausage with four legs'?" "What if you changed these two sentences around?"

Read your partner's selection. Use *EQS* to fill in the boxes.

Name _____ Partner's Name _____

E: Encourage	*Q*: Question	*S*: Suggestions

Writing to Succeed

Deductive and Inductive Reasoning

Deductive reasoning is "deductive" because you make a point or thesis and use your speaking or writing to prove your point with specific facts. You end with a conclusion.

Inductive reasoning is different. You start by stating or writing some key facts, then tying them up together at the very end. Instead of proving your thesis statement, you are building it. This is good when you start writing a presentation with a certain conclusion in mind.

Summary: Deductive speaking and writing begins with a generalization or statement and then gives facts and evidence that lead to a conclusion. Inductive speaking and writing begins with specific facts that lead to a conclusion.

Choosing Exact Words

Exact words make your writing vivid, precise, and interesting.

Sentence with General Words	Sentence with Exact Words
He **walked** into the **room, smiled,** and **said,** "Guess what? I got a raise at work!"	He **strolled** into the **kitchen, grinned broadly,** and **announced,** "Guess what? I got a raise at work!"

Paragraph Organization

A **paragraph** is a group of sentences about a topic. In informational texts and persuasive writing, a paragraph usually has a topic sentence and supporting details for the idea in that topic sentence. The topic sentence is often, but not always, at the beginning of a paragraph.

A longer piece of writing, such as a narrative, may have many paragraphs. These paragraphs are divided into three parts: the introduction, the body, and the conclusion.

A longer piece of writing usually has a thesis statement. This is like a "topic sentence" for the entire piece. The paragraphs give support for the thesis statement.

Paragraph

1. Write in a notebook or on the computer.
2. Write a topic sentence, supporting details, and a closing sentence.
3. Use a dictionary or computer software for help with words and spelling.

Title

Indent

(Topic Sentence)

(Details, Supporting Facts, Examples)

(Closing Sentence: topic sentence with different words)

Narrative

Draft

➤ Use this graphic organizer when you write your first draft. Use transition words.

Title Page

Title
Name
Date

Beginning

Indent   **Introduction**

Indent   **Body**

Middle

Indent

Indent

End

Indent   **Conclusion or Resolution**

Persuasive Essay

Five Paragraphs

➤ Use this graphic organizer for oral presentations or writing assignments.

1. Write in a notebook or on the computer.
2. Write a thesis stating your position.
3. Give three reasons with examples and a conclusion.
4. Use words such as *first of all, next, finally,* and *in conclusion.*
5. Use a dictionary or computer software to help with words and spelling.

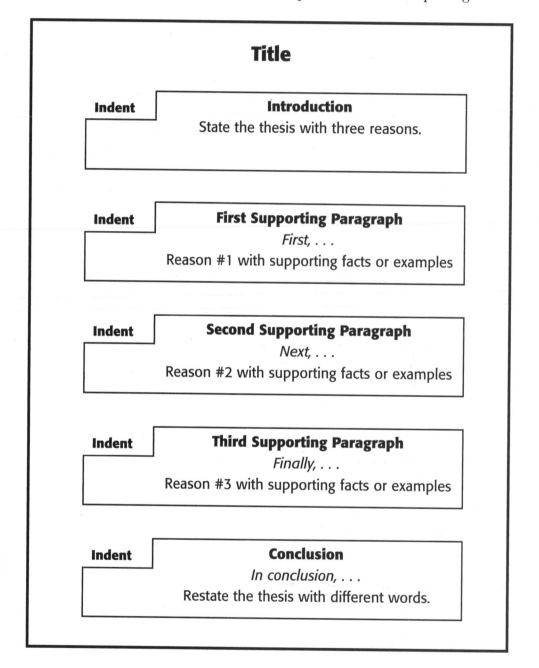

Title

Indent | **Introduction**
State the thesis with three reasons.

Indent | **First Supporting Paragraph**
First, . . .
Reason #1 with supporting facts or examples

Indent | **Second Supporting Paragraph**
Next, . . .
Reason #2 with supporting facts or examples

Indent | **Third Supporting Paragraph**
Finally, . . .
Reason #3 with supporting facts or examples

Indent | **Conclusion**
In conclusion, . . .
Restate the thesis with different words.

VISIONS Student Handbook • Copyright © Heinle

Persuasive Checklist

Use this checklist to evaluate your own writing and your classmates' writing.

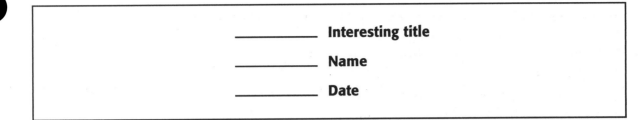

_____ **Interesting title**

_____ **Name**

_____ **Date**

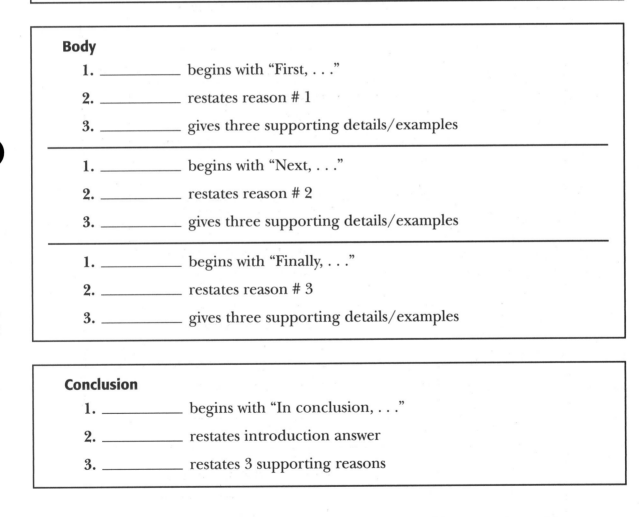

Introduction

1. _____ asks a question

2. _____ answers a question

3. _____ gives 3 supporting reasons for answer

Body

1. _____ begins with "First, . . ."

2. _____ restates reason # 1

3. _____ gives three supporting details/examples

1. _____ begins with "Next, . . ."

2. _____ restates reason # 2

3. _____ gives three supporting details/examples

1. _____ begins with "Finally, . . ."

2. _____ restates reason # 3

3. _____ gives three supporting details/examples

Conclusion

1. _____ begins with "In conclusion, . . ."

2. _____ restates introduction answer

3. _____ restates 3 supporting reasons

_____ I used the Editor's Checklist to edit and revise this persuasive writing.

Friendly Letter

➤ This format is used for writing a letter to a friend.

1. Write on an 8½ by 11 inch piece of paper or on personal stationery.
2. Write using good penmanship.
3. Proofread your spelling and punctuation.

_____
(Date)

Dear _____ ,

Indent

Describe yourself and where you are.

Indent

Describe your daily life.

Indent

Talk about the person you are writing to.

Yours truly,

(Your name)

Business Letter/Letter to the Editor

➤ A business letter is different from a friendly letter. It is brief, direct, and limited to one or two points. It is appropriate to type a business letter on a word processor or computer.

1. In the first paragraph, clearly state what you want or why you are writing.
2. Add supporting information in the second paragraph.
3. Write a polite closing.
4. If possible, use a computer for your final draft.
5. Proofread for spelling, grammar, capital letters, and proper business form.

Your Street
City, State/Country
Date

Company Name
Address

Dear _____ :

Indent Why are you writing?

Indent Explain what you introduced in the first paragraph.

Indent Closing (Conclusion)

Sincerely,

(signature)

The Research Process

Identify Topic and References

Step 1. Identify a topic.

Be sure that your topic is specific, not general. It is difficult to research and write about a general topic.

General Topics →	Specific Topics
Rain Forests →	The Climate of Rain Forests Why Rain Forests Are Important Ways to Save the Rain Forests
My Family →	My Grandparents' Funny Wedding Sunday Dinner at Home What Drives My Parents Crazy

Step 2. Write questions about your topic.

Your questions guide your research. As you find out information, you will write new questions and revise your original questions.

Step 3. Use references.

Find out more about your topic by using a variety of reference resources. Here is a list of resources in your school or community library. Use the Table of Contents or index to help you find what you need.

Reference	Description	How to Use It
Encyclopedias	Articles on thousands of topics	Book encyclopedias: Topics are in alphabetical order and have cross-references to other related topics and information.
	Many illustrations, photos, charts, and maps	CD-ROM or online encyclopedias: Type in keywords and then click on the articles.
The Internet	Internet Web pages on all kinds of topics	Type in keywords in a browser. Follow the links to sites that seem useful to you.
The library	Books	Type keywords in the library's catalog. Ask the librarian to help you find the books you want.
	Magazines, newspapers, almanacs, books of lists, indexes	Ask the librarian to help you find what you need. Current issues are usually on display. Reference books may not be checked out of the library.
Experts	People who know about your topic	Interview experts. Prepare your questions ahead of time.

VISIONS Student Handbook • Copyright © Heinle

Step 4. Make note cards.

Note cards help you keep track of the facts you find and their sources. Use note cards to organize your information when you start to write. See page 22.

1. Record the facts that answer your questions on note cards. Each note card should contain three parts.
2. Record the reference citations like this:

Type of Reference	Citation
Books	Author. <u>Title of Book.</u> City of Publication: Publisher, Year. **Example:** Roper, Edward R. <u>Rain Forest.</u> New York: Omni Publishing, 1998.
Magazines	Author. "Title of Article." <u>Title of Magazine</u> Date: Page(s). **Example:** Tyler, Dawn. "On the Sands." <u>Hawaii Living</u> Feb. 1998: 20–23.
Encyclopedias	Author of Article. (if given) "Article Title." <u>Title of Book.</u> City of Publication: Publisher, Year. **Example:** Alpert, Louis C. "Inca." <u>Encyclopedia Americana.</u> International Edition. 1999.
Web sites	Creator's name (if given). <u>Web Page Title.</u> Institution or organization. Date of access <URL network address>. If you cannot find the information, use the web address as the citation. **Example:** Likakis, Angela. "The World of Science." <u>Science News</u> 28 Feb. 1998: 137. Science Resource Center. InfoSci. Boston Community College. 6 Nov. 2000 <http://infosci.thinkgroup.com/itweb/boston_massachusetts>.

Step 5. Write your research paper.

1. Organize your notes in logical sequence. You may not want to use all of them.
2. Use transitions to blend your sentences and paragraphs. Revise and rearrange text as needed.
3. Incorporate visuals.

Step 6. Create a bibliography and a Table of Contents.

1. At the end of your writing, start a new page with the title "Bibliography."
2. List all of the references that you used to write your report, using the citations from your note cards. Put them in alphabetical order.
3. Do not list references that you read but did not use in your report.
4. Make a Table of Contents to show the organization of your report. List the page numbers of each section.

Note-Taking

Research Report

1. Use 4 x 6 inch cards.
2. Use a variety of resources: encyclopedias, the Internet, books, magazines, software resources, experts, etc.
3. Think of three or four questions about the topic.
4. Write each question at the top of a different note card.
5. Paraphrase an idea or copy a "quotation" on each card.
6. In the bottom left-hand corner, identify the source and page number.
7. In the upper right-hand corner, write the general heading of the information.

Question: _____   **General Heading:** _____
(What do you want to know?)

Paraphrase your source.

or

Summarize from your source.

or

"Quote" your source.

Source, page

Outline

Informational Texts and Research Papers

1. Sort your note cards before you do your outline.
2. Organize topics and subtopics into logical order.
3. Keep it simple. Write a topic or a thesis—not complete sentences.
4. List major headings after a Roman numeral and a period.
5. List subtopics after a capital letter and a period.
6. List supporting details and examples after a number and a period.

Title

I. Topic 1 or Thesis
   A. Subtopic 1
      1. Detail/Example
      2. Detail/Example

   B. Subtopic 2
      1. Detail/Example
      2. Detail/Example

II. Topics or Thesis
   A. Subtopic 1
      1. Detail/Example
      2. Detail/Example

   B. Subtopic 2
      1. Detail/Example
      2. Detail/Example

III. Conclusion (Restate thesis)

Final Draft

```
┌─────────────────────────┐
│                         │
│          Title          │
│                         │
│          Name           │
Title Page │   Date          │
│                         │
└─────────────────────────┘
```

Thesis (in opening paragraph)
A statement that clearly and briefly says why you chose this topic to research.

Topic (the two to three subtopics you researched)
The information should be relevant to the topic.

Subtopic 1
Start a new page.

Subtopic 2
Start a new page.

Conclusion
A paragraph that summarizes your report and tells how your research helped you reach the goals of your purpose.

---

1. **Visuals:** You may want to include pictures, graphs, tables, or photos
2. **Bibliography:** Check with your teacher for a copy of the correct format required for a bibliography. Also see page 21 for correct reference citation.
3. **Format:** If you use a computer, double space and use 12–14 point font with one inch margins around the paper. If you write by hand, use black or blue pen and cursive writing.
4. **Proofread:** Check for spelling and grammar mistakes. Remember that computer software spell check only catches words that are spelled incorrectly. It does not catch words that are spelled correctly but used incorrectly.

VISIONS Student Handbook • Copyright © Heinle

Research Paper Checklist

Use this checklist to guide your research and evaluate your research paper.

Research

_____ 1. I formed interesting questions about my subject.

_____ 2. I researched my questions in references, such as periodicals and the Internet, or I asked experts.

_____ 3. I took notes on information and ideas from these sources.

_____ 4. I revised my research questions and added new ones as needed.

_____ 5. I organized my information and ideas, for example, in an outline or a web.

_____ 6. I used at least three sources to prove my topic sentence or thesis.

Sources

_____ 1. I evaluated each reference source for credibility.

_____ 2. I did not plagiarize. I summarized, paraphrased, or quoted my sources.

_____ 3. I documented sources for all information that is not my own opinion.

_____ 4. If I used exact words from a source, I put them in quotation marks and said where they came from.

Organization

_____ 1. I stated my thesis question clearly in the introduction.

_____ 2. I stayed focused on my topic and thesis.

_____ 3. I included three sentences that support my thesis and elaborated on these sentences.

_____ 4. I used transitional words (_First, Next, Then, Finally..._) to blend ideas, events, and paragraphs.

_____ 5. I summarized and answered my thesis question in the conclusion.

Writing

_____ 1. I used the active voice whenever possible.

_____ 2. I checked my spelling with the computer's spell check.

_____ 3. I checked my punctuation in every sentence.

_____ 4. I checked my choice of words to make sure I said what I wanted to say.

_____ 5. I checked my verb tenses and subject-verb agreement.

Form

_____ 1. I wrote an interesting title that reflects the subject.

_____ 2. I wrote my name and date on the first page.

_____ 3. I double-spaced my paper on the computer.

_____ 4. I checked the margins on each page and numbered each page.

_____ 5. I indented each paragraph.

_____ 6. I capitalized the first word of each sentence and all proper nouns.

_____ 7. I documented my sources correctly, in the style assigned.

_____ 8. I integrated quotations into my paper correctly.

_____ 9. I did a final proofreading.

Evaluation

_____ 1. I thought about how well I answered my research questions.

_____ 2. I thought about questions for further research.

Technology

The Computer

You can use a computer to help you work. You can also use a computer to help you find information. A computer is made up of **hardware** and **software.** Hardware is the part of the computer that you can touch. Software is the instructions that make the computer work.

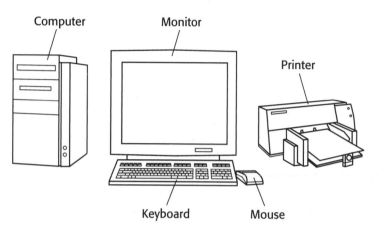

Computer   Monitor   Printer   Keyboard   Mouse

Computer Hardware

1. The most important part of a computer is the box that contains the computer's memory. Your information is stored in the computer's memory.
2. You give information to the computer by typing on a keyboard and by clicking a mouse.
3. You see the information on the monitor. The monitor looks like a television screen.
4. You can use a printer to print the information on paper.

Computer Software

Software is made to do a special kind of job. For example, there is software that helps you write and edit your writing (word processing). There is software that makes it easy to create presentations. Other software lets you find information on the Internet. These pieces of software are also called **programs** or **applications.**

Word Processing

A word processing program is a tool for writing. You can use it to:

- correct mistakes, move text around, and add or delete text
- do spelling and grammar checks to help you find and correct errors
- find synonyms by using a thesaurus in the program
- create visuals
- choose text features such as **boldface type** and *italic type*

➤ How to Create a Document

Anything that you write in a word processing program is called a **document.**

1. Make sure that the computer is on.
2. Find the **icon** (the little picture) for your word processing program on the screen.
3. Use the mouse to move the arrow and click on the program to open it. Different computers do this in different ways. Ask someone to help you.
4. When the program opens, you can start typing.
5. You can learn how to use special keys on the keyboard. For example, if you press the key marked **Tab** when you are at the beginning of a line, the computer will make a paragraph indentation. The **Shift** keys make capital letters.

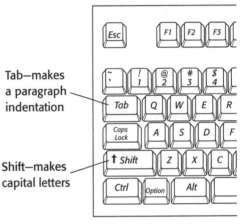

Tab—makes a paragraph indentation

Shift—makes capital letters

Look at the icons in this illustration. You can click on these icons with the mouse to make special effects such as **bold** or *italic* type. (The icons on your program might be different from these.)

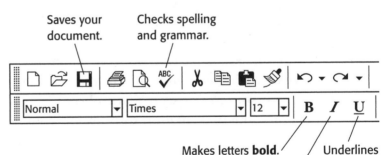

Saves your document.

Checks spelling and grammar.

Makes letters **bold**.
Makes letters *italic*.

Underlines letters.

6. VERY IMPORTANT: The computer will not "remember" your work by itself. You have to save your work in the computer's memory. There is usually an icon that will make the computer do this. The computer will ask you to name your document. As you write, save your work often.

When you have finished your first draft, use the spelling and grammar checks to find and fix errors. You can add text features and visuals if you like. Print your work or send it to someone by E-mail.

Technology Presentations

Using media such as videos, graphics, and slides on a computer can make your oral presentations clearer and more interesting.

Step 1. Plan the media parts of your presentation.
1. Plan, organize, and prepare your presentation. See Steps 1–3 on page 1. Take notes on how technology could help make your points.
   a. Is there a video that would help show your idea? Could you make one?
   b. Would music add to your presentation? What kind? Where can you get it?
   c. Should you show charts and visuals on the computer?
2. Make note cards. Use one card for what you will say and another card for the technology parts. Put the cards in order.

Card 1 My speech:	Card 2 Media:	Card 3 My speech:
Sports	Play video of sports scenes in town	Sports are fun
Important in our community		Teamwork
Most people like some kind of sport		Healthy
Introduce video		

Step 2. Prepare the media parts of your presentation.
1. Find or create the images and sounds that you want to use. Look in the "Clip Art" section of your software or scan art or photos into your program.
2. If available, use the presentation software on your computer to organize them.

Step 3. Practice your presentation.
1. Practice your technology presentation using Step 5 on page 1.
2. Ask a partner to watch your presentation and use the Speaking Checklist on page 2.

Step 4. Give your technology presentation to your audience.
1. Set up your equipment early to be sure that everything is working.
2. After your presentation, ask the audience to complete the Active Listening Checklist on page 3.

VISIONS Student Handbook • Copyright © Heinle

How to Use the Internet

➤ **Key Definitions**

Internet	millions of computers connected together to exchange information
Web sites	locations on the Internet
browser	software that lets you see Web sites
keywords	words that describe a topic
link	takes you to another Web site or to another place in the same Web site when you click your mouse on it

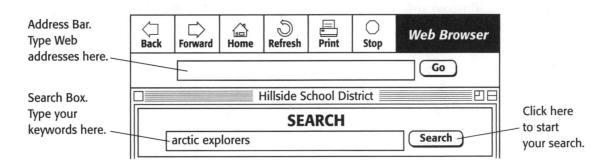

Address Bar. Type Web addresses here.

Search Box. Type your keywords here.

Click here to start your search.

➤ **Do Research on the Internet**

1. Open your browser. Ask your teacher or a classmate how to do this.
2. Type keywords for your topic in the "search" box. Click on the button that says "go" (or "start" or "search").
3. Look at the list of Web sites that comes up on the screen. Choose one of the sites that seems interesting and click on it.
4. On a Web site, there are pages of information. Sometimes there are links to take you to other Web sites.
5. If you already know the exact address of a Web site, you can type it into the address bar. For example, http://visions.heinle.com.

```
  ⟵      ⟶      ⌂       ↻       🖶       ◯      Web Browser
 Back  Forward  Home  Refresh  Print   Stop

 [                                          ]  ( Go )

 ☐ ▤▤▤▤▤▤▤    Hillside School District   ▤▤▤▤ ◰◱

            SEARCH
 [ arctic explorers                    ]  ( Search )

 Arctic Explorers-EnchantedLearning.com – AMUNDSEN,ROALD
 (1872–1928) was a Norwegian polar explorer who was first person…

 High Arctic Explorers – The first Arctic explorers, of course, were the
 Inuit themselves. …

 Arctic Explorers – What are some good pictures for your poster? What
 kind of hardships and obstacles…

 Arctic Explorers – These sites are about the Arctic and the explorers of
 the area. …
```

Links are underlined. Click on a link to go to that site.

➤ **Use Information from the Internet**

Many Web sites have good information. Others may have mistakes or they may tell only one side of an issue. You must evaluate the information that you find on the Internet. Ask your teacher or another adult for suggestions of sites that you can trust. Use other resources to check the information you find on the Internet.

How to Use E-Mail

➤ **Key Definitions**

E-mail	software that lets you type a message and send it to someone else who has E-mail
E-mail address	where the E-mail system sends the message
inbox	the place in your E-mail software where E-mail messages are received and read

➤ **Read an E-Mail Message**

1. Open the E-mail program. Ask your teacher or a classmate how to do this. See if there are any new messages in your inbox.
2. Open a message. Programs do this differently. Usually you double click the mouse on the message.
3. Read the message.
4. If you want to keep the message, do not do anything. The computer will save it in your inbox. If you want to discard the message, click on the delete button on the toolbar.
5. To send an answer back, click on the reply button. Write your message and click "send."

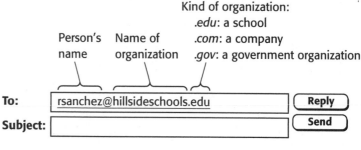

Person's name Name of organization

Kind of organization:
.edu: a school
.com: a company
.gov: a government organization

To: rsanchez@hillsideschools.edu [Reply]
Subject: [Send]

➤ **Send an E-Mail Message**

1. Open your E-mail program.
2. On the toolbar, click on the new message button.
3. Type in the address of the person you are writing to.
4. Type in a subject that tells what the message is about.
5. Type your message.
6. Click on the "send" button.

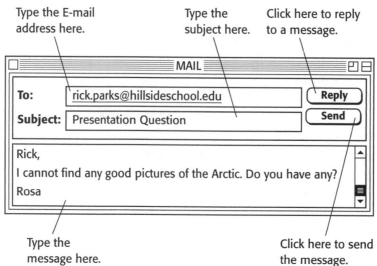

Type the E-mail address here.   Type the subject here.   Click here to reply to a message.

MAIL

To: rick.parks@hillsideschool.edu   [Reply]
Subject: Presentation Question   [Send]

Rick,
I cannot find any good pictures of the Arctic. Do you have any?
Rosa

Type the message here.   Click here to send the message.

VISIONS Student Handbook • Copyright © Heinle

Grammar and Usage

Parts of Speech: Nouns

➤ **What is a Noun?**

A **noun** is a word that names a person, a place, or a thing.

Person	Place	Thing
teacher	home	desk

➤ **Singular and Plural Nouns**

If a noun names *one* person, place, or thing, it is a **singular** noun.
If a noun names *more than one* person, place, or thing, it is a **plural** noun.
Make the plural of most nouns by adding *-s* to the singular form.

Singular		Plural	Example
teacher	+ **-s**	teacher**s**	I like my teachers.

➤ **Special Spelling of Some Plural Nouns**

Noun Ending In	Rule	Examples
-s, -ch, -sh, -x	Add *-es*	bus → bus**es**, church → church**es**, brush → brush**es**, box → box**es**
-f or *-fe*	Change *-f* or *-fe* to *-ves*	knife → kni**ves** loaf → loa**ves**
a consonant + *-y*	Change *y* to *i* and add *-es*	penny → penn**ies**
a consonant + *-o*	For some nouns, just add *-s* For other nouns, add *-es*	piano → piano**s** tomato → tomato**es**

➤ **Some Irregular Plural Nouns**

Singular	Plural	Singular	Plural
child	children	mouse	mice
fish	fish	sheep	sheep
foot	feet	tooth	teeth
man	men	woman	women

➤ **Count and Noncount Nouns**

You can count the fingers on your hand, but you cannot count the water in a glass. *Finger* is a **count noun**. *Water* is a **noncount noun**.

➤ **Expressions of Quantity That Are *Different* for Count and Noncount Nouns**

Count Nouns	many	We do not have many apples.
	few	I need a few apples.
Noncount Nouns	much	We do not have much water.
	a little	I need a little water.

➤ **Expressions of Quantity**

Expressions of quantity tell *how much* or *how many*. Some of these expressions are different for count and noncount nouns.

➤ **Possessive Nouns**

A **possessive noun** tells who owns or has something.

Yang's *sister walks to school with him.*

(Yang has a sister. She walks to school with him.)

1. Make the possessive form of most nouns by adding **'s** to a singular noun or **'** to a plural noun ending in *-s*.

	Noun	Possessive	Example
Singular	friend	friend**'s**	My friend's house is next door.
Plural	friends	friend**s'**	All my other friends' houses are far away.

2. If a noun has an irregular plural, add **'s**.

Singular	Plural	Example
man	men	The men's room is over there.

VISIONS Student Handbook • Copyright © Heinle

Parts of Speech: Articles

There are three articles: *a, an,* and *the.* Articles are used with nouns.

➤ **Definite Article** *The*

1. Use the article *the* for a specific noun.

   *I do not usually like rice, but **the rice** your mother cooks is great.*

2. You can use *the* with singular and plural count nouns and before noncount nouns.

➤ **Indefinite Articles** *A* **and** *An*

1. Use *a* and *an* with singular count nouns when the noun is indefinite or your audience does not know about it.

   *I have **a brother** and **a sister.***

2. Use *a* before a word beginning with a consonant sound. Use *an* before a word beginning with a vowel sound.

   *I have **a cousin.** I also have **an uncle.***

➤ **No Article**

You can use a plural count noun or a noncount noun without an article, when you talk about things in general.

   *I love **roses.***   *(count)*

   ***Snow** is beautiful.*   *(noncount)*

➤ **Special Rules for Names of Places**

1. Do not use *the* before continents, countries, states, and cities.

   *She is from **Dallas.***

   ***South America** is very large.*

   Exception: *the* United States

2. Use *the* with regions of countries that are directions.

   *New York is in **the Northeast.***

   *It gets very hot in **the South.***

3. Use *the* before names of mountains, lakes, and islands that are plural.

   ***The Caribbean Islands** are beautiful.*

4. Do not use *the* with mountains, lakes, and islands that are singular.

   ***Puerto Rico** has great beaches.*

5. Use *the* with bodies of water and deserts.

   ***The Pacific Ocean** is the largest ocean in the world.*

Parts of Speech: Pronouns

A **pronoun** takes the place of a noun that has already been mentioned or that is understood.

My brother was late to school today because **he** missed the bus. *(he = my brother.)*

➤ **Subject Pronouns**

Subject pronouns are used mostly as the subjects of sentences.

He missed the bus.

	Singular	Plural
First person	I	we
Second person	you	you
Third person	he/she/it	they

➤ **Object Pronouns**

Objects pronouns come after a verb to show who (or what) something happened to, or who got something.

We caught some fish, and my mother cooked **them.**

Object pronouns come after prepositions.

When my friends left, I left with **them.**

	Singular	Plural
First person	me	us
Second person	you	you
Third person	him/her/it	them

➤ **Possessive Pronouns**

Possessive pronouns tell who owns or has something.

Is that your book or **mine**?

	Singular	Plural
First person	mine	ours
Second person	yours	yours
Third person	his/hers/its	theirs

➤ **Reflexive Pronouns**

Reflexive pronouns show that the object in a sentence is the same person or thing as the subject.

I hurt **myself** playing basketball.

	Singular	Plural
First person	myself	ourselves
Second person	yourself	yourselves
Third person	himself/herself/itself	themselves

Subject-Verb Agreement

➤ **Basic Agreement**

The **subject** and **verb** in a sentence must agree in number. When a **subject** is **singular,** the **verb** must be **singular.** When the **subject** is **plural,** the **verb** must be **plural.** The present tense of the third-person singular ends in -*s*.

	Singular	Plural
First person	I eat	we eat
Second person	you eat	you eat
Third person	he/she/it eat**s**	they eat

VISIONS Student Handbook • Copyright © Heinle

➤ **Agreement with Be**
The verb *be* is special. It does not follow the usual agreement verb pattern.

Forms of *Be*			
Present Tense		**Past Tense**	
Singular	**Plural**	**Singular**	**Plural**
I **am**	we **are**	I **was**	we **were**
you **are**	you **are**	you **were**	you **were**
he/she/it **is**	they **are**	he/she/it **was**	they **were**

➤ **Agreement of Compound Subjects**
Use a plural verb with most compound subjects (two or more subjects) joined by the word *and*. The present tense of the verb does not have *-s* or *-es* added to it.

She *and* her friends **spend** lots of time together.
Swimming *and* running **help** him stay in shape.

Parts of Speech: Adjectives

Adjectives describe people, places, or things.

describes the ball   describes the boy   describes the park
↓   ↓   ↓
We gave a **big** ball to the **little** boy in the **beautiful** park.

➤ **Comparative Adjectives**
Comparative adjectives plus *than* compare two things.

Olga is 17. Her brother Ivan is 15. Olga is **older than** Ivan.

➤ **Spelling Rules for Comparative Adjectives**
1. **Short adjectives**
Add *-er* to an adjective to make the comparative form and then use *than*.

Adjective Ending In	Rule	Examples
the letter *e*	add *-r*	wide → wide**r** than
one vowel and one consonant	double the consonant and add *-er*	hot → hot**ter** than
a consonant and the letter *y*	change the *y* to *i* and add *-er*	happy → happ**ier** than
all other short adjectives	add *-er*	warm → warm**er** than

2. **Longer adjectives**
Use the word *more* before a longer adjective, and *than* after it.

My sister is **more serious than** I am.

➤ **Superlative Adjectives**

When you compare three or more things, use *the* plus the superlative adjective form.

Jules is five feet tall. Marta is five feet, four inches tall. Yang is six feet tall.
Yang is **the tallest.**

➤ **Spelling Rules for Superlative Adjectives**

1. **Short adjectives**

Add -*est* to the adjective to make the superlative form.

Adjective Ending In	Rule	Examples
the letter *e*	add -*st*	wide → wide**st**
one vowel and one consonant	double the consonant and add -*est*	hot → hot**test** sad → sad**dest**
a consonant and the letter *y*	change the *y* to *i* and add -*est*	happy → happ**iest**
all other adjectives	just add -*est*	warm → warm**est**

2. **Longer adjectives**

Use the word *most* before a longer adjective.

My sister is **the most serious** person in her class.

3. **Irregular comparative and superlative forms**

Adjective	Comparative Form	Superlative Form
good	better than	the best
bad	worse than	the worst

VISIONS Student Handbook • Copyright © Heinle

Parts of Speech: Verbs

A **verb** expresses an action or state of being of the subject of the sentence. Every complete sentence must have a subject and a verb.

➤ **Subject + Action Verb + Object(s)**
1. Some action verbs can be followed by a **direct object.**
   A verb followed by a direct object is called a **transitive verb.**

Subject	Action Verb	Direct Object
We	do	our homework.
Fire	burns	wood.

2. Some action verbs can be followed by two objects, a direct object and an indirect object. The **indirect object** tells who or what received the direct object.

Subject	Action Verb	Indirect Object	Direct Object
My dad	gives	me	money.

➤ **Subject + Action Verb**
   Some action verbs are not followed by objects. These are called **intransitive verbs.**

Subject	Verb
The train	stops.
We	stopped.

➤ **Subject + State of Being Verb + Complement**
1. State of being verbs include *be* and verbs like *seem, become, sound, feel, look, taste,* and *smell.*
2. A complement can be a noun or an adjective. A complement gives more information about the subject of a sentence.

Subject	State of Being Verb	Complement
I	am	tired.
You	look	happy.
The food	smells	good.

➤ **The Simple Present Tense**
Use the simple form of the verb. Add *-s* for third-person subjects.

Subject	Verb	Use
I/You/We/They	work.	To say that something is generally true *I* **work** *hard.* To say that something happens regularly. *I* **work** *every Saturday.*
He/She/It	work**s**.	*She* **works** *harder.* *She* **works** *every Sunday.*

➤ **The Simple Past Tense**
Add *-ed* to the simple form of the verb.

Subject	Verb	Use
I/You/He/She/It/We/They	work**ed**.	To say that something happened in the past and it is finished *I* **worked** *all day yesterday.*

1. To make simple past tense questions, use *did* plus the simple present tense form of the verb.

   Did you **work** *yesterday?*

2. To make simple past tense negative statements, use *did not* plus the simple tense form of the verb.

   I **did not work** *all day yesterday.*

3. The contraction form for *did not* is *didn't*.
4. For irregular past tense verbs, see the chart on page 41.

➤ **The Simple Future Tense**
Use *will* with the simple form of the verb.

Subject	Verb	Use
I/You/He/She/It/We/They	**will** + work	To make strong predictions about the future *I* **will work** *to get good grades.*

1. To make questions, put *will* before the subject.

   Where **will** *you* **be** *tomorrow morning?*

2. To make negative statements, put *not* after *will*.

   They **will not (won't) like** *this movie.*

3. The contraction forms are: *will* → *'ll, will not* → *won't*.

   He **'ll** *call tomorrow. He* **won't** *call today.*

VISIONS Student Handbook • Copyright © Heinle

➤ **The Present Progressive Tense**
Use the verb *be* plus the *-ing* form of the verb.

Subject	Verb	Use
I	**am** work**ing**.	To say that something is happening now and is not finished
He/She/It	**is** work**ing**.	*She **is working**.*
You/We/They	**are** work**ing**.	

1. To make a question, put *am, is,* or *are* before the subject.
*What **are** you **doing** now?*

2. To make a negative sentence, use *not* after *am, is,* or *are.*
*They **are not (aren't) doing** their homework now. OR They**'re not doing** their homework now.*

3. The contractions often used are: are → *'re,* is → *'s,* am → *'m.*
I'm working. He's working. They're working.

➤ **The Past Progressive Tense**
Use *was* or *were* plus the *-ing* form of the verb.

Subject	Verb	Use
I/He/She/It	**was** work**ing**.	To say that something was happening and not finished at a point in the past
You/We/They	**were** work**ing**.	*I **was working** at 9:00.*

1. To make a question, put *was* or *were* before the subject.
***Was** he working?*

2. To make a negative sentence, use *not* after *was* or *were.*
*I **was not** working.*

3. Contractions are often used for *was not* and *were not.*
*I **wasn't** working. They **weren't** working.*

➤ **The Future Progressive Tense**
Use *will be* plus the *-ing* form of the verb.

Subject	Verb	Use
I/You/He/She/It/We/They	will be work**ing**.	To say that something will be going on and not finished at a point in the future *They **will be** working until 6:00.*

1. To make questions, put *will* before the subject.
***Will** you **be working** tomorrow?*

2. To make negative sentences, put *not* after *will.*
*They **will not be working** tomorrow.*

3. The contraction forms are: *will* → *'ll, will not* → *won't.*
*I'll be working tomorrow. He **won't** be working tomorrow.*

➤ The Present Perfect Tense

Use *have* or *has* with the past participle of the verb.

Subject	Verb	Use
I/You/We/They	**have** work**ed**.	To talk about something that started in the past and continues in the present *I **have worked** here since 2004.*
He/She/It	**has** work**ed**.	To talk about something that happened in the past but is important to the present *She **has worked** in Mexico, so she speaks Spanish well.*

1. To make a question, put *have* or *has* before the subject.
   ***Have** you worked here a long time?*
2. To make a negative sentence, put *not* after *have* or *has*.
   *I **have not** worked here for a long time.*
3. The contraction forms are: ***has** → 's, **have** → 've.*
   ***He's** worked here one year.*   ***I've** worked here a long time.*

➤ The Past Perfect Tense

Use *had* with the past participle of the verb.

Subject	Verb	Use
I/You/He/She/It/They	**had worked**.	To say that something happened before something else *I **had worked** there for two months before school started.*

1. To make a question, put *had* before the subject.
   ***Had** he worked before he came here?*
2. To make a negative, put *not* after *had*.
   *I **had not** worked very long when the bell rang.*
3. The contraction form is: ***had** → 'd.*
   ***I'd** worked before he was born.*

➤ The Future Perfect Tense

Use *will have* with the past participle of the verb.

Subject	Verb	Use
I/You/He/She/It/They	**will have worked**.	Use the future perfect tense to say that something will happen before something else or before a time in the future. *Next month, I **will have worked** here for two years.*

1. To make a question, put *will* before the subject.
   ***Will** you **have finished** your work by noon?*
2. To make a negative, put *not* after *will*.
   *I **will not have** finished by 11:00.*
3. The contraction forms are: ***will** → 'll, **will not** → won't.*
   ***I'll have** finished my work before I go out. He **won't have** finished.*

➤ Irregular Verbs
Some verbs are irregular. Their simple past forms and past participles do not end in -ed.

Some Common Irregular Verbs

Simple Form	Simple Past	Past Participle
become	became	become
begin	began	begun
bite	bit	bitten
break	broke	broken
bring	brought	brought
build	built	built
buy	bought	bought
catch	caught	caught
choose	chose	chosen
come	came	come
cost	cost	cost
do	did	done
draw	drew	drawn
drink	drank	drunk
drive	drove	driven
eat	ate	eaten
fall	fell	fallen
feed	fed	fed
feel	felt	felt
fight	fought	fought
fly	flew	flown
forget	forgot	forgotten
freeze	froze	frozen
get	got	gotten
give	gave	given
go	went	gone
grow	grew	grown
have	had	had
hear	heard	heard
hit	hit	hit
hold	held	held
hurt	hurt	hurt
keep	kept	kept
know	knew	known
lay	laid	laid

Simple Form	Simple Past	Past Participle
leave	left	left
lend	lent	lent
lie	lay	lain
lose	lost	lost
make	made	made
mean	meant	meant
pay	paid	paid
put	put	put
read	read	read
ride	rode	ridden
run	ran	run
say	said	said
see	saw	seen
sell	sold	sold
send	sent	sent
shake	shook	shaken
shut	shut	shut
sing	sang	sung
sit	sat	sat
sleep	slept	slept
speak	spoke	spoken
spend	spent	spent
stand	stood	stood
steal	stole	stolen
sweep	swept	swept
swim	swam	swum
take	took	taken
teach	taught	taught
tear	tore	torn
tell	told	told
think	thought	thought
throw	threw	thrown
understand	understood	understood
win	won	won
write	wrote	written

Phrasal verbs have two or three words. Phrasal verbs often have special meanings.

➤ **Intransitive Phrasal Verbs**

Some phrasal verbs do not take objects.

Phrasal Verb	Meaning	Example
grow up	get older, mature	*She **grew up** in Phoenix.*
take off	leave the ground	*The plane **takes off** at noon.*

➤ **Transitive Phrasal Verbs**

1. Transitive phrasal verbs have an object.

   *I will **turn on** the television.*

2. With some phrasal verbs, the object can come in the middle of the phrasal verb.

   *I will **turn** the television **on**.*

   *I will **turn** it **off**.*

3. In some transitive phrasal verbs, the object must always go after the phrasal verb.

   *We will **go over** the homework together.*

Common Phrasal Verbs: Transitive		
ask for	get along with	put up with
call back	get off	run into
call off	go on	show off
call on	go over	take back
call up	hand in/out	take off
cheer up	look for	throw out
clean up	look into	turn down
come in	look over	turn off
fill in	pick up	wake up
fill out	put away	
find out	put on	

Common Phrasal Verbs: Intransitive	
come back	look out
eat out	pass away
get up	show up
go back to	sit down
go out	sit up
grow up	stand up

➤ Modal Verbs
Modal verbs add meaning to verbs.

*Pete **can** work very fast.*

The modal verb *can* says that Pete *is able to* work very fast.

➤ Form of Modal Verbs
All modal verbs are used with the simple form of the action
or state of being verb.

Subject	Modal Verb	Simple Verb
I/You/He/She/It/We/They	**can**	**work** fast.

➤ Present and Future Tense Modal Verbs

Meaning	Modal Verb	Example
Express ability	can	*He **can** work hard.*
Express possibility	may might could	*I **may** work tomorrow if I feel better.* *He **might** be able to work tonight.* *This radio does not work. It **could** need batteries.*
Give advice	should	*She **should** go to sleep early.*
Give orders or rules	must	*You **must** work on your grammar.*
Make an inference	must	*You **must** work hard if you want to succeed.*
Ask for and give permission	may can	***May** I work over the weekend?* *You **can** work tomorrow instead of Friday.*

➤ Past Modal Verbs

Meaning	Past Form	Example
Express ability	**could** + simple form	*I **could** work ten hours a day when I was young.*
Express possibility	**may/might/could** + **have** + past participle	*I **may have done** it. (I cannot remember.)* *I **might have done** it, if she had asked me.* *I **could have done** it when you were here.*
Give advice	**should** + **have** + past participle	*You **should have eaten** breakfast.*
Give orders or rules	**had to** + simple verb	*We **had to be** on time.*
Make an inference	**must** + **have** + past participle	*The boys are not here. They **must have gone** home.*

Parts of Speech: Adverbs

Adverbs describe verbs, adjectives, or other adverbs. They often answer the question "how?"

*The man spoke **softly**.* (The adverb *softly* describes the verb *spoke*.)

*The audience was **surprisingly** large.* (The adverb *surprisingly* describes the adjective *large*.)

*She wrote **very** quickly.* (The adverb *very* describes the adverb *quickly*.)

Many adverbs are made of an adjective + *-ly*, for example:

Adjective	+ -ly	Adverb
quick	add **-ly**	quick**ly**
happy	change **y** to **i**, add **-ly**	happ**ily**
simple	drop **e**, add **ly**	simp**ly**

Be careful when using **good** and **well**. *Good* is an adjective. *Well* is an adverb.

*That is a **good** band.* (The adjective **good** describes the noun *band*.)

*The band plays **well**.* (The adverb **well** describes the verb *played*.)

Parts of Speech: Prepositions

Prepositions and the words that follow them can tell *where*, *when*, and *how* something happens.

*They woke up **at** 6 A.M.* (The preposition **at** tells when they woke up.)

*She is playing **in** the park.* (The preposition **in** tells where she is playing.)

*Mary walks **with** energy.* (The preposition **with** tells how she walks.)

A **prepositional phrase** is a preposition and the words that follow it.

*She put the plate **on the table**.* (**On the table** is a prepositional phrase.)

Common Prepositions		
about	below	of
above	between	on
against	by	over
around	for	through
at	from	to
before	in	under

Parts of Speech: Conjunctions

Conjunctions can join two clauses (parts of a sentence with a subject and a verb).

Coordinating conjunctions join two independent clauses (clauses that can stand alone).

independent clause   independent clause
Maria did her homework, and I helped her.

Common Coordinating Conjunctions
and, or, but, so

Subordinating conjunctions join an independent clause (a clause that can stand alone) with a dependent clause (a clause that cannot stand alone). For more about clauses, see page 46.

independent clause   dependent clause
I lived in Haiti before I came here.

Some Subordinating Conjunctions

Conjunction	Use	Example
when	Tells when something happened	*I lived in Haiti **before** I came here.*
before		***Before** I came here, I lived in Haiti.*
after		
because	Gives a reason	*He took the job **because** he wanted the experience.* ***Because** he wanted the experience, he took the job.*
although	Shows a contrast	*She walks to school **although** her home is two miles away.* ***Although** her home is two miles away, she walks to school.*

Sentence Types

➤ **Clauses**

Sentences are made of **clauses.** Clauses have at least one subject and one verb.

subject verb

Raoul read the book.

1. Some clauses are **independent clauses.** They can stand alone as a sentence.

Raoul read the book.

2. Other clauses are **dependent clauses.** Dependent clauses cannot be sentences by themselves. They must be used with an independent clause.

dependent clause   independent clause

While he was in bed, Raoul read the book.

➤ **The Three Sentence Types**

	Feature	Example
Simple Sentence	one independent clause	Raoul read the book.

	Feature	Example
Compound Sentence	two independent clauses joined by a conjunction like and, but, or so	Raoul read the book, **and** he understood it.

	Feature	Example
Complex Sentence	an independent clause and a dependent clause joined by a subordinating conjunction like after, although, because, before, if, once, since, until, unless, when, while	Raoul read the book **because** it was assigned for homework.
	an independent clause and a dependent clause joined by a relative pronoun like that, who, which, whose, where	Raoul read the book **that** the teacher assigned.

VISIONS GRAMMAR AND USAGE

VISIONS Student Handbook • Copyright © Heinle

Word Study

Common Greek and Latin Word Roots

Common Greek Word Roots		
Root	**Meaning**	**Key Word**
aster	star	astronaut
auto	self	automatic
biblio	book	bibliography
bio	life	biology
chron	time	chronology
geo	earth	geology
hemi	half	hemisphere
mech	machine	mechanic
meter	measure	speedometer
micro	small	microscope
mono	single	monorail
para	beside	parallel
phon	sound	phonograph
psych	mind, soul	psychic
scope	see	microscope
sphere	ball	hemisphere
syn	together	synonym
tele	from afar	telephone
therm	heat	thermometer

Common Latin Word Roots		
Root	**Meaning**	**Key Word**
aud	hear	audio
bene	well, good	benefit
centi	hundred	centipede
contra	against	contrary
dict	say, speak	dictate
duct	lead	conduct
equi	equal	equitable
extra	outside	extravagant
fac	make	factory
fig	form	figure
form	shape	formula
fract	break	fraction
init	beginning	initial
ject	throw	reject
junct	join	junction
man	hand	manual
miss	send	missile
pop	people	popular
port	carry	transport
rupt	break	erupt
sign	mark	signal
spect	look	inspect
struct	build	construct
trac/tract	pull	tractor
urb	city	urban
vid/vis	see	video/visual
voc	voice	vocal
volv	roll	revolve

VISIONS WORD STUDY

Most Frequent Prefixes and Suffixes

Prefixes			
Prefix	**Meaning**	**Example**	**Origin**
anti-	against	antifreeze	Latin
auto-	self	automobile	Latin
bi-	two	bicycle	Latin
de-	opposite	defrost	Latin
dis-	not, opposite of	disagree	Latin
en-, em-,	cause	encode, embrace	Latin
fore-	before	foreshadow	Latin
hyper-	over	hyperactive	Greek
in-, im-	in	infield	Latin
in-, im-, il-, ir-	not	injustice, impossible	Latin
inter-	between	interact	Latin
mid-	middle	midway	Latin
mis-	wrongly	misfire	Latin
non-	not	nonsense	Latin
over-	over	overlook	Latin
pre-	before	prefix	Anglo-Saxon
re-	again	return	Latin
semi-	half	semicircle	Latin
sub-	under	submarine	Latin
super-	above	superstar	Latin
trans-	across	transport	Latin
un-	not	unfriendly	Latin
under-	under	undersea	Anglo-Saxon

Suffixes			
Suffix	**Meaning**	**Example**	**Origin**
-able, -ible	can be done	comfortable	Latin
-al, -ial	having characteristics of	personal	Latin
-en	made of	wooden	Latin
-er, -or	one who	worker, actor	Anglo-Saxon
-ful	full of	careful	Anglo-Saxon
-ic	having characteristics of	linguistic	Latin
-ing	verb form/present participle	running	Anglo-Saxon
-ion, tion, -ation, -ition	act, process	occasion, attraction	Latin
-ist	one who	dentist	Greek
-ity, -ty	state of	infinity	Latin
-less	without	fearless	Anglo-Saxon
-ment	action or process	enjoyment	Latin
-ness	state of, condition of	kindness	Anglo-Saxon
-ology	study of	biology	Greek
-ous, -eous, -ious	possessing the qualities of	gaseous	Anglo-Saxon

VISIONS Student Handbook • Copyright © Heinle

Word Study and Spelling

Keep a list of new words that you learn. Use a dictionary, a glossary, or the Newbury House Dictionary CD-ROM to find definitions.

Word	Page	Sentence from Reading	Definition	Your Sentence

Writing Conventions

Spelling

Here are some general rules about English spelling. If you are unsure of how to spell a word, it is best to check it in a dictionary.

ie and *ei*	Example
1. Use *i* before *e* except after *c*. 2. Use *i* before *e* except when letters are pronounced *ay* as in *eight*.	**<u>*i* before *e*</u>** **<u>*ei* after *c*</u>** *chief* *friend* *receive* *ceiling* **<u>*ei* pronounced *ay*</u>** *weigh* *freight* *neighbor* *eight*
q and *u*	Example
Always place the letter *u* after the letter *q*.	*May I ask a* **qu***ick* **qu***estion before we begin the* **qu***iz?*
Plurals	Example
1. Add *-es* to words that end in *s, ss, sh, ch, x,* and *z*. 2. If a word ends in a consonant plus *y*, change the *y* to *i* and add *-es*. 3. For all other words, just add *-s*.	*We washed the dish***es** *after supper.* *Bab***ies** *need a lot of care.* *She collects baseball hat***s***.*
y **Before a Suffix**	Example
1. Change the letter *y* to an *i* and add *-ed, -er, -es,* or *-est* if a word ends in a consonant plus *y*. 2. Do not change the *y* to an *i* if you add *-ing* to a verb. 3. Just add *-ed* or *-s* to words that end in a vowel plus *y*.	*The blue room is pretty.* *The yellow room is prett***ier** *than the blue room.* *We are study***ing** *for our exam tomorrow.* *The boys and girls play***ed** *in the playground.*
Doubling Final Consonants	Example
For one-syllable words with one vowel that end in one consonant, double the last consonant before you add an ending.	*Will he drop the bag?* *The boy dro***pp***ed the bag on the floor.* *The red ball was the bi***gg***est of the three.*
Silent *e* Before a Suffix	Example
1. Keep the silent *e* when a suffix that begins with a consonant is added to a word, for example, *-ful, -ness,* or *-ment*. 2. Drop the silent *e* when a suffix that begins with a vowel is added to a word, for example, *-ed, -es, -ing, -er,* or *-est*.	*The school was hop***eful** *that their team would win.* *The puppy is very liv***ely***.* *I hop***ed** *we would see each other.* *We are liv***ing** *in an apartment right now.*
-able, -ible	Example
1. If the root of a word is an independent word, the suffix *-able* is usually used. 2. If the root of a word is not an independent word, the suffix *-ible* is usually used.	<u>independent:</u> *comfort***able***, agree***able***, dry***able*** <u>dependent:</u> *compat***ible***, incred***ible***, plaus***ible***

Punctuation and Capitalization

Punctuation and capitalization help the reader to understand meaning. Use punctuation marks and capital letters when you write so your reader can understand your message.

1. Use a period (.)	Example
at the end of a statement	I went to school today.
at the end of a command	Take Exit 12 to the school.
after an abbreviation	Ave., Mr., St., Dr.
after an initial	Frank R. Pacheco

2. Use a question mark (?)	Example
at the end of a question	Who is that man?

3. Use an exclamation point (!)	Example
at the end of a sentence to show strong feeling	Look at that great color!
at the end of strong commands	Shut that door!
after interjections	Oh!

4. Use an apostrophe (')	Example
to show possession	The girl's jacket was hanging in the closet. The students' books are here.
in a contraction	He's = <u>He is</u>, isn't = <u>is not</u>, didn't = <u>did not</u>

5. Use quotation marks (" ")	Example
to show someone's exact words	"Your table is ready," the waiter said.
around exact words taken from a book, newspaper, or other print resource	According to today's newspaper, the weather will be "sensational."
around titles of articles in magazines, newspapers, and journals	The article, "Tips to Help You Write Better," in that magazine was very interesting.
around titles of essays, short stories, short poems, and songs	The title of my favorite short story is "The Circuit."
around titles of chapters or sections of books	The title of Unit 6 is "Freedom."

6. Use a comma (,)	Example
to separate three or more items in a series	Red, yellow, and blue are colors.
between two or more adjectives that describe the same noun	She drank the cold, delicious lemonade.
before a direct quotation	The man said, "Turn left at the next light."
between the day and year in a date	July 4, 1776
between city and state	Dallas, Texas
after the opening of a friendly letter	Dear Marie,
after the closing of a letter	Sincerely, Michael
before an appositive	Our teacher, Mr. Garcia, is very nice.
before the coordinating conjunction in a compound sentence	I want to go shopping, but Lara wants to watch a movie.
in long numbers, after every three digits from the right	5,000 1,250,000

7. Use a colon (:)	Example
to start a list. It follows a complete sentence.	A good student does the following things: attends class, studies hard, and completes all assignments.

8. Use a semicolon (;)	Example
to show a close relationship between two complete sentences	The department store does not sell tools; the hardware store does.
to separate two complete sentences that are joined by a transitional word or phrase	I will pick you up at work; however, I may be a little late.
to separate a series of words or phrases that already have commas in them	On our trip, we visited Boston, Massachusetts; Chicago, Illinois; and San Francisco, California.

9. Use parentheses ( )	Example
around extra, or nonessential, information in a sentence	It is so cold out today (15° Fahrenheit) that I think I will stay inside.

10. Use a hyphen (-)	Example
to divide a word at the end of a line. Always divide the word between syllables.	Antonio forgot the girl's name. He was embarrassed.
to form some compound words	His five-year-old son is very good at reading.
to connect words in a number	There are twenty-eight students in that class.

Capitalization	Example
Capitalize the first word in a sentence.	We took a class trip.
Capitalize the pronoun I.	John and I are best friends.
Capitalize the first word in a direct quotation.	Marie said, "They are getting on the bus."

Capitalize proper nouns, including	Example	
names of specific people	George Washington	
names of specific places	Cities and States	New York City, NY
	Countries	Mexico
	Continents	Asia
names of specific things	Days and Months	Saturday
	Holidays	Thanksgiving
	Special Events	Olympics
	Nationalities	American
	Languages	Spanish
	Religions	Christianity
	Organizations	Math Club
	Businesses	West High School
abbreviations of proper nouns	Titles	Dr. (Doctor)
	Words in Addresses	St. (Street)
important words in a title	We read the book *The Call of the Wild.*	

VISIONS Student Handbook • Copyright © Heinle

Handwriting: Print Letters

Handwriting: Cursive Letters

Test-Taking Tips

Use these tips to help you improve your performance on tests.

BEFORE THE TEST

1. Complete all of your assignments on time.

2. Take notes in class as you go over your assignments.

3. Save and review your class notes, assignments, and quizzes.

4. Ask your teacher what topics will be covered on the test.

5. Ask your teacher what kind of test you will take. For example, will the questions be true/false, multiple choice, or essay?

6. Be organized. Make a study guide. Making note cards or rewriting information will help you review.

7. Study, and then get a good night's sleep before the test.

8. Eat a good, healthy breakfast on the day of the test.

9. Bring everything that you need to the test (pencils, erasers, pens).

DURING THE TEST

1. Pay close attention to the teacher's instructions. Ask questions if you do not understand.

2. Read the instructions on the test carefully.

3. Look at the test before you begin to see how long it is.

4. Don't spend too much time on any one section or question. Skip questions that you don't know. Return to them if you have time at the end.

5. Watch the time to make sure you finish the whole test.

6. Save time to look over the test before you turn it in. Don't worry if other students finish before you. Use all the time that you have.

AFTER THE TEST

1. When your test is returned to you, look at it carefully.

2. Look up the answers to any questions you left blank or got wrong.

3. Ask your teacher about any questions that you still don't understand. The same question might appear again on another test.

⇨

TYPES OF TEST QUESTIONS

TRUE/FALSE STATEMENTS

Decide if the following statement is *true* or *false*.

> _____ *False* _____ **1.** All trees lose their leaves in the winter.

1. Read the statements carefully.
2. Look for anything in the statement that is not true. If any detail is false, then the whole statement is false.
3. Watch out for absolute words like *always, all, never, no, best,* and *worst.* These may be clues that the statement is false.

MULTIPLE-CHOICE QUESTIONS

Choose the correct answer from the list of choices.

> **1.** Which type of tree loses its leaves in the fall?
>   **a.** coniferous tree   **b.** pine tree   **©.** deciduous tree   **d.** fir tree

1. Read the question carefully before you look at the answer choices.
2. Answer the question before you look at the choices. Then see if your answer is listed.
3. Read all of the answers before you choose one.
4. If you are not sure which answer is correct, cross out the ones that you know are wrong. Choose one of the answers that is left.

ESSAY QUESTIONS

Write one or more paragraphs to answer the question.

> **1.** Describe three things that happen to deciduous trees in the fall.

1. Know what you are being asked to do (for example, *describe, discuss, compare, explain,* and so on).
2. Plan your essay before you begin to write. Making a basic outline first will help you stay focused.
3. Include a *thesis statement, supporting evidence,* and a *conclusion.*
4. Show how much you know, but stay focused. Include only information that is relevant to your topic or thesis.
5. Write neatly. Your teacher must be able to read your answer.

VISIONS Test-Taking Tips

Glossary of Terms

adjective	An **adjective** describes a noun (a person, place, or thing).
adverb	**Adverbs** describe **verbs** (words that show action). Many adverbs end in -*ly*.
antonym	An **antonym** is a word that has an opposite meaning to another word.
autobiography	An **autobiography** is the story of a person's life, written by that person.
biography	A **biography** is the story of a person's life, written by another person.
cause and effect	A **cause** is the reason why something happens. An **effect** is an event that happens as a result of the cause.
characters	**Characters** are the people in a story.
character motivation	**Motivation** is the reason why a character does something.
character traits	**Character traits** suggest how a character feels or what a character is like.
chronological order	**Chronological order** is the order in which events really happen.
clause **main clause** **dependent clause**	A **clause** is part of a sentence that has a subject and a verb. A **main (independent) clause** can stand alone as a complete sentence. A **dependent clause** cannot stand alone as a sentence and must always be used with a main clause.
compare	To **compare** (or to **make a comparison**) is to see how two or more things are the same.
compound word	A **compound word** is the combination of two words into one larger word. You can usually figure out the meaning of a compound word if you look at each part separately.
conclusion	A **conclusion** is the ending of a piece of writing. [derived from *conclude: to end*]
conjunction	A **conjunction** is a word like *and, but,* and *so.* Conjunctions can join two sentences or parts of sentences.
connotative meaning	**Connotative meanings** are feelings and attitudes connected to a word. Example: home = comfort, security, fun.
context	Sometimes you can guess the meanings of new words by using the **context,** or nearby words and sentences.
contrast	To **contrast** is to show how two or more things are different.
denotative meaning	**Denotative meanings** are the literal definitions found in a dictionary. Example: the place where one lives
description	**Description** is the details of a person, place, thing, or event. Writers often use description to help readers make pictures in their minds (mental images). [derived from *describe*]
details	The **details** of a reading include all the information that helps you understand the main idea.

dialogue	The **dialogue** of a story is the exact words the characters say.
diary	A **diary** is a book in which you record your experiences and private thoughts every day.
draw a conclusion	When you decide that something is true, or not true, after thinking carefully about all the facts, you **draw a conclusion.**
fable	A **fable** is a story in which the main characters are usually animals that act like humans. A fable usually teaches a **moral** (a lesson about life).
fiction	**Fiction** is a type of story that has made-up characters and events.
figurative language	To make their stories more interesting, writers often describe one thing by comparing it to another thing. This is called **figurative language.**
first-person narrative	In a **first-person narrative,** the writer uses a person in the story to tell the story, using the pronouns *I, me, we,* and *us.*
flashback	A part of a story in which the order of events is interrupted by the telling of an event from the past.
foreshadowing	**Foreshadowing** gives clues about what is going to happen in a story. [derived from *fore: before* + *shadow*]
genre	/ˈʒɑnrə/ The kind of literature is the **genre,** for example, poetry, a short story, or a play.
glossary	A **glossary** is a part of a book that gives the meanings of difficult words.
historical nonfiction narrative	A **historical nonfiction narrative** tells the story of a real event.
historical fiction	**Historical fiction** is a made-up story set during a time in history. This kind of story combines made-up people and events with real characters and events that really happened.
homonym	**Homonyms** are words that are pronounced and spelled the same, but have different meanings.
homophone	**Homophones** are words that are pronounced the same, and may have different spellings, but have different meanings. Example: be, bee. [derived from Greek *homo: same* + *phone: sound*]
idiom	**Idioms** are expressions (sayings) that have meanings different from the exact meanings of the words.
images	Writers use words that help readers create **images** (pictures) in their minds.
inference	To make an **inference** is to make a guess using what you know. [derived from *infer: to guess*]
interview	An **interview** is made up of questions and answers between two people.

VISIONS Student Handbook • Copyright © Heinle

introduction	An **introduction** is the beginning of a piece of writing. [derived from *introduce*]
journal	A **journal** is a book in which you record your daily experiences and special events. It is written for other people to read.
legend	A **legend** is a story that has been passed down from generation to generation. It is often based on real events and real people, but parts of the story are usually made up or exaggerated.
main idea	The **main idea** of a paragraph or of a longer part of a reading is the most important idea of that part of a reading.
memoir	In a **memoir** /ˈmɛmˌwɑr/, the writer tells about events in his or her distant past.
metaphor	A **metaphor** is figurative language which describes something by showing how it is like something else. [from Greek *meta: with* + *pherein: to carry*]
mood	**Mood** is the feeling the writer wants a reader to get from the text.
myth	A **myth** /mɪθ/ is a made-up story told from one generation to the next. Many myths explain something in nature and tell about events that could never happen in real life.
narrative	A **narrative** is a piece of writing that is in the form of a story.
narrator	A **narrator** is the person who tells a story. [derived from *narrate: to tell*]
nonfiction	**Nonfiction** is writing that tells about real people and events. Nonfiction writing includes **facts** (information that is true).
noun	A **noun** is a person, a place, or a thing.
personification	**Personification** gives human thoughts, feelings, and actions to an object or an animal. [derived from *personify: to make like a human*]
persuasive writing	In **persuasive writing,** the author wants the reader to believe something. Writers of persuasive text use **facts** (information that is true) to support their **opinions** (beliefs about something). [derived from *persuade: to convince*]
play	In a **play,** actors speak lines before an audience. They pretend to be the characters in the play.
plot	The **plot** is the series of main events that makes up a story.
poetry	**Poetry** is creative writing usually made up of **stanzas** (groups of lines). Poetry may have words that rhyme at the end of each line. **Poets** (writers of poetry) often express feelings and include description to help readers create mental **images** (pictures in their minds).
point of view	**Point of view** is the relationship of a storyteller to the story. It can also refer to someone's opinion.
predict	A reading often includes clues that you can use to **predict,** or guess, what you think will happen next.

VISIONS GLOSSARY OF TERMS

prefix	A **prefix** is a group of letters that is added to the beginning of a word. It may change the meaning of a word.
proper nouns	**Proper nouns** are the names of people, specific places, and some time words (*Tuesday, January*). The first letter in a proper noun is capitalized.
realistic fiction	**Realistic fiction** is a story that includes made-up characters and events that could happen in real life.
repetition	**Repetition** is the repeating of words and ideas in a piece of writing. [derived from *repeat: to say or do again*]
rhyme	Words that **rhyme** have the same ending sound.
root	The main part of a word is the **root.** You can sometimes understand the meaning of a word by looking at the root.
science fiction	**Science fiction** is a made-up story that is based on **scientific facts** (information from science that is true). The setting of a science fiction story often takes place in the future or in a place that might be real according to science. The plot often combines events that seem impossible with events that might happen according to science.
setting	**Setting** is the time and place in which the events of a story happen.
short story	A **short story** develops the characters, plot, and resolution in a few pages.
simile	A **simile** is figurative language that uses the words *like* or *as* to compare two things.
simple verb	A **simple verb** is a verb with no endings or other changes. For example, *walk, speak,* and *see* are simple verbs.
simple present tense	The **simple present tense** describes things that are generally true or happen regularly.
stanza	A **stanza** is a group of lines in a poem.
style	**Style** is the way something is written. It includes word choice, **mood** (the feeling the reader gets from a reading), and **tone** (the way the writer thinks and feels about a reading).
suffix	A **suffix** is a group of letters that is added to the end of a word and may change the meaning of a word or its part of speech.
summary	A **summary** tells the most important information of a reading.
synonym	A **synonym** is a word that has a similar meaning to another word.
theme	**Theme** is what a piece of writing is about.
thesaurus	A **thesaurus** /θəˈsɔrəs/ is a book or software that groups words together into **synonyms** (words that have similar meanings), and **antonyms** (words that have opposite meanings).
tone	**Tone** is the writer's attitude (way of thinking and feeling) toward the subject and characters.
transitions	**Transitions** are words or groups of words that connect sentences and ideas.

VISIONS Student Handbook • Copyright © Heinle